C000064782

Year 3

Excellence in Problem Solving Mathematics

Hilary Koll and Steve Mills

RISING STARS

Rising Stars UK Ltd.

7 Hatchers Mews, Bermondsey Street, London, SE1 3GS

www.risingstars-uk.com

Every effort has been made to trace copyright holders and obtain their permission for the use of copyright materials. The authors and publisher will gladly receive information enabling them to rectify any error or omission in subsequent editions.

All facts are correct at time of going to press.

Text, design and layout © Rising Stars UK Ltd.

The right of Hilary Koll and Steve Mills to be identified as the authors of this work has been asserted by them in accordance with the Copyright, Design and Patents Act 1998.

Published 2010

Authors: Hilary Koll and Steve Mills

Design and typesetting: Sally Boothroyd

Editorial: Bruce Nicholson, Ruth Burns

Artwork: Sally Boothroyd, Michael Emmerson, David Woodroffe

Cover Design: Words and Pictures

Photo acknowledgements
p.11 *tennis balls* © Aleksey Khromov/iStockphoto; **p.13** *coconut* © Rafał Ulicki/iStockphoto; **p.32** *parcel* © winterling/iStockphoto, *package tied with string* © david franklin/iStockphoto; **p.34** 3D *movie* © James Blinn/iStockphoto; **p.43** *archery board* © naphtalina/iStockphoto

All rights reserved. No part of this publication may be reproduced, stored in a retrieval system, or transmitted, in any form by any means, electronic, mechanical, photocopying, recording or otherwise, without the prior permission of Rising Stars.

British Library Cataloguing in Publication Data.

A CIP record for this book is available from the British Library.

ISBN: 978-1-84680-761-9

Printed by Craft Print International Ltd, Singapore.

Contents

	Using and applying mathematics					Counting and understanding number				Knowing and using number facts		
	Solve one- and two-step problems involving numbers, money or measures, including time; choosing and carrying out appropriate calculations	Represent the information in a puzzle or problem using numbers, images or diagrams; use these to find a solution and present it in context, where appropriate using £.p notation or units of measure	Follow a line of enquiry by deciding what information is important; make and use lists, tables and graphs to organise and interpret the information	Identify patterns and relationships involving numbers or shapes and use these to solve problems	Describe and explain methods, choices and solutions to puzzles and problems, orally and in writing, using pictures and diagrams	Read, write and order whole numbers to at least 1000 and position them on a number line; count on from and back to zero in single-digit steps or multiples of 10	Partition three-digit numbers into multiples of one hundred, ten and one in different ways	Round two- or three-digit numbers to the nearest 10 or 100 and give estimates for their sums and differences	Read and write proper fractions, e.g. $\frac{3}{7}$, $\frac{9}{10}$, interpreting the denominator as the parts of a whole and the numerator as the number of parts; identify and estimate fractions of shapes; use diagrams to compare fractions and establish equivalents	Derive and recall all addition and subtraction facts for each number to 20, sums and differences of multiples of 10 and number pairs that total 100	Derive and recall multiplication facts for the 2, 3, 4, 5, 6 and 10 times-tables and the corresponding division facts; recognise multiples of 2, 5 or 10 up to 1000	Use knowledge of number operations and corresponding inverses, including doubling and halving, to estimate and check calculations
Patterns and sequences	✔	✔		✔	✔	✔						
Addition and subtraction	✔	✔		✔	✔					✔		✔
Multiplication	✔	✔		✔	✔						✔	✔
Division and remainders	✔	✔		✔	✔						✔	✔
Mixed calculations	✔	✔		✔	✔					✔	✔	✔
Fractions	✔	✔	✔	✔	✔				✔			
Money	✔	✔		✔	✔							
Place value	✔	✔		✔	✔	✔	✔					
Number lines and rounding	✔	✔		✔	✔	✔		✔				
Measures – length	✔	✔		✔	✔							
Measures – capacity	✔	✔		✔	✔							
Measures – mass	✔	✔		✔	✔							
Time	✔	✔		✔	✔							
2-D shapes	✔	✔		✔	✔							
3-D shapes	✔	✔		✔	✔							
Position and direction	✔	✔		✔	✔							
Tables	✔	✔	✔	✔	✔							
Graphs, charts and diagrams	✔	✔	✔	✔	✔							

	Calculating						Understanding shape				Measuring			Handling data	
	Add or subtract mentally combinations of one- and two-digit numbers	Develop and use written methods to record, support or explain addition and subtraction of two- and three-digit numbers	Multiply one- and two-digit numbers by 10 or 100, and describe the effect	Use practical and informal written methods to multiply and divide two-digit numbers, e.g. 13 × 3, 50 ÷ 4; round remainders up or down, depending on the context	Understand that division is the inverse of multiplication and vice versa and use this to derive and record related multiplication and division number sentences	Find unit fractions of numbers and quantities, e.g. $\frac{1}{2}, \frac{1}{3}, \frac{1}{4}$ and $\frac{1}{6}$ of 16 litres	Relate 2-D shapes and 3-D solids to drawings of them; describe, visualise, classify, draw and make the shapes	Draw and complete shapes with reflective symmetry and draw the reflection of a shape in a mirror line along one side	Read and record the vocabulary of position, direction and movement, using the four compass directions to describe movement about a grid	Use a set-square to draw right angles and to identify right angles in 2-D shapes; compare angles with a right angle; recognise that a straight line is equivalent to two right angles	Know the relationships between kilometres and metres, metres and centimetres, kilograms and grams, litres and millilitres; choose and use appropriate units to estimate, measure and record measurements	Read, to the nearest division and half-division, scales that are numbered or partially numbered; use the information to measure and draw to a suitable degree of accuracy	Read the time on a 12-hour digital clock and to the nearest five minutes on an analogue clock; calculate time intervals and find start or end times for a given time interval	Answer a question by collecting, organising and interpreting data; use tally charts, frequency tables, pictograms and bar charts to represent results and illustrate observations; use ICT to create a simple bar chart	Use Venn diagrams or Carroll diagrams to sort data and objects using more than one criterion
Patterns and sequences	✔														
Addition and subtraction	✔	✔													
Multiplication			✔	✔	✔										
Division and remainders				✔	✔										
Mixed calculations	✔	✔	✔	✔	✔										
Fractions						✔									✔
Money	✔	✔	✔	✔	✔										
Place value			✔												
Number lines and rounding															
Measures – length	✔	✔									✔	✔			
Measures – capacity	✔	✔									✔	✔			
Measures – mass	✔	✔									✔	✔			
Time													✔		
2-D shapes							✔	✔							
3-D shapes							✔								✔
Position and direction									✔	✔					
Tables														✔	
Graphs, charts and diagrams														✔	

5

How to use this book

This book is designed to help you use your mathematical skills to solve a range of problems, many of which are written in words rather than figures.

Rather than giving a calculation like:

$4 \times 6 = \boxed{}$

a word problem might be something like:

If I have 4 six-packs of cola, how many cans of cola do I have in total?

The answer is the same, but you need to think about it a bit more and remember to answer by writing or saying: *I have 24 cans of cola in total.*

The introduction

This section of each page gives you an idea of the sort of problems you are likely to see and helps you to understand what maths you need to use.

Mixed calculations

It is important to be able to work out whether to add, subtract, multiply or divide to find the answer to a word problem.

In a field there are cows, sheep and horses. There are 10 more sheep than cows. There are half as many horses as cows. If there are 16 sheep, how many cows and how many horses are there?

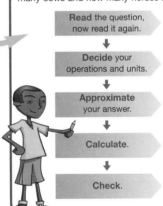

Read the question, now read it again.	Read slowly and carefully. What are you being asked to do?
Decide your operations and units.	I need to take 10 from 16 to find the number of cows and then halve the answer to find the number of horses.
Approximate your answer.	16 – 10 is 6 and half of 6 is 3, so I think there are 6 cows and 3 horses.
Calculate.	16 – 10 = 6 so there are 6 cows. 6 ÷ 2 = 3 so there are 3 horses.
Check.	I'll re-read the question to make sure my answers fit. I'm right!

Hints and tips

Some questions will have just one step and others may have more. Think carefully about what to do and read the question carefully to the end.

The example problem

The flow chart takes you through an example problem step-by-step. This is important when answering word problems as it helps you to order your thoughts, do each part of the problem in the right order and check your work!

Every problem has the same five steps:

READ the question, then read it again

DECIDE your operations and units

APPROXIMATE your answer

CALCULATE

CHECK your answer

We can remember this by using this mnemonic:

Rain

Drops

Are

Crystal

Clear

Hints and tips

The Hints and tips section gives you useful ideas for completing the problems on the opposite page. These are the things you need to remember if you are doing a quiz or test.

The questions

The questions get harder as you go down the page.

- Section 1 questions are fairly straightforward and help you to practise your skills.

- Section 2 questions are a bit harder. They will help you to remember all the key points.

MIXED CALCULATIONS

Questions

1
a) A farmer has 8 chickens. If each lays 3 eggs, how many eggs is this altogether?

b) The farmer puts the eggs into boxes of 6. How many boxes this?

c) Jess the sheepdog rounds up 17 sheep and puts them in a field that already has 39 sheep in. How many sheep are in the field now?

2
a) There are twice as many goats as pigs and half as many pigs as geese. If there are 8 goats, how many geese are there?

b) In a field there are cows, sheep and horses. There are twice as many sheep as cows. There are half as many horses as cows. If there are 16 sheep, how many cows and how many horses are there?

c) A pond has a total of 52 ducks and ducklings. There are 10 more ducklings than ducks on the pond. How many ducklings are there?

CHALLENGE.
On Julian's farm there are 36 sheep, 40 cows, 6 pigs and 9 chickens. Write three questions of your own about Julian's farm for a partner to answer.

Challenge

The Challenge is really tough and sometimes involves making up games and your own questions.

Explore   Find out how a sheep's fleece can be turned into wool. Can you find more information about carding and spinning? Draw and label some diagrams to show the process.

19

Explore

This section gives you a chance to investigate the topic in more depth and to make links with other subjects. You may be asked to write about something or do some research.

Ten top tips for working with word problems

1 *Work step-by-step.* Follow the flow chart.

Rain   **Read** the question, now read it again.

⬇

Drops   **Decide** your operations and units.

⬇

Are   **Approximate** your answer.

⬇

Crystal   **Calculate**.

⬇

Clear   **Check**.

2 Always *show your working* or 'method'. This will help you to keep track of what you have done and may help you to get extra marks.

3 Always *include the units* in your answer. If you don't, you won't get full marks.

4 When you first read through a question, *underline important words and numbers*. This will help you to remember the important bits.

5 *Draw a picture to help you.* Sometimes a question is easier if you can 'see' it. For example, drawing 6 apples can help you if you need to divide them.

6 If the problem has a number of steps, break it down and do *one step at a time*.

7 To *check your answers*, look at the inverse operation.

8 Sometimes an answer will 'sound right'. Read it out (quietly) and listen. *Does it make sense?*

9 If you are using measurements (grams, litres, cm), make sure that the *units are the same* before you calculate.

10 Once again! *Read the question again and check that your solution answers it.*

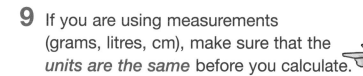
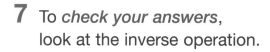

Patterns and sequences

Most sequences go up or down in equal-sized steps. Find out the size of the step and count forwards or backwards to find the missing number or numbers in the pattern.

A man walks seven kilometres (km) each day. Continue this pattern to find how far he walked in six days.

| 7 km | 14 km | 21 km | 28 km | 35 km | ? |

 Read the question, now read it again.

Read slowly and carefully. What are you being asked to do?

 Decide your operations and units.

I need to add another 7 km to 35 km to continue the pattern.

 Approximate your answer.

35 + 10 = 45, so the answer will be a bit less than 45.

 Calculate.

35 km + 7 km = 42 km

Check.

I can count back 7 from 42 to see if the answer is 35. Yes, I was correct!

Hints and tips

Sometimes a number is missing from the middle of a sequence. You can count forwards or backwards from the number either side of it.

Questions

1 a) A flower grows 3 cm each day.
Continue the pattern to show
how tall it has grown after 7 days.

   3 cm   6 cm   9 cm   12 cm   15 cm   18 cm   ?

b) Granny keeps adding scoops of flour onto some scales.
Each scoop of flour weighs 100 g. What is the next number
in this pattern?

   400 g   500 g   600 g   700 g   800 g   900 g   ?

c) What is the missing number in this sequence?

   2   7   12   17   22   ?   32   37

2 a) What are the three missing numbers in this sequence?

   32   29   ?   23   20   ?   14   ?

b) The Olympic Games takes place every four years.
What are the missing years in this sequence?

   1980   1984   1988   1992   ?   2000   2004   ?   2012

CHALLENGE!

Make up three of your own number
sequences that start with the
number 2 and have the number 20
somewhere in the sequence.

Explore

Find out about and draw some shape sequences
that match number sequences, like this one.

      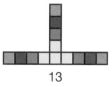

4   7   10   13

Draw a shape sequence for the sequence 5, 9, 13, 17.

Addition and subtraction

For many word questions you find answers by adding or subtracting. Use the number facts that you know to help you or use mental methods to work out the answer.

A ghost train can hold 48 children. There are already 39 children on the train. If 5 more children get on the ghost train how many more children could it hold?

Read the question, now read it again.

⬇

Decide your operations and units.

⬇

Approximate your answer.

⬇

Calculate.

⬇

Check.

Read slowly and carefully. What is the question asking?

I need to take 39 and 5 from 48. That is subtracting.

39 is about 40, so $48 - 40 = 8$ and $8 - 5$ is 3, so the answer will be near to 3.

$48 - 39 - 5 = 48 - 44 = 4$ The train could hold 4 more children.

I can add 4, 5 and 39 to see if I get 48. Yes, I was correct!

Hints and tips

When adding, you can use subtraction to check your answer.
When subtracting, you can use addition to check your answer.

Questions

 1 a) There were 44 people in the hall of mirrors. 19 more people went in. How many people are now in the hall of mirrors?

b) There were 62 people on the big wheel. 26 people got off. How many people are now on the big wheel?

c) A ride can hold 55 people. If there are 37 people on the ride, how many more people can it hold?

 2 a) There were 65 people on a roller coaster. 32 people got off and 9 more people got on. How many people are now on the roller coaster?

b) The difference between an adult ticket price and a child's ticket price is £8. If the adult ticket is £17, how much is the child's ticket?

c) A stick of candy floss costs 99p. Rumi has 38p and her Dad gives her 50p. How much more money does she need to buy one stick of candy floss?

CHALLENGE! Using the numbers 9, 12, 15 and 16, add three of them together and subtract the fourth number. Which different numbers can you make?

What is special about all the numbers you can make?

Explore

Have you ever been to a funfair? Write about your favourite ride. Why is it your favourite? What was good about it? Was it good value for money?

Multiplication

For some word problems you need to use multiplication to find the answer. Use your times tables to work out the answers.

A sports shop sells tennis balls in packs of 3 or 4.
A tennis club buys five packs of 3 balls and
four packs of 4 balls.
How many balls does the club buy altogether?

Read the question, now read it again.	Read slowly and carefully. What are you being asked to do?
Decide your operations and units.	I need to find 5 lots of 3 and 4 lots of 4 and add the answers.
Approximate your answer.	I know that $5 \times 3 = 15$ and $4 \times 4 = 16$. Double 15 is 30, so the answer will be just over 30.
Calculate.	$5 \times 3 = 15$ and $4 \times 4 = 16$ $15 + 16 = 31$ The answer is 31 balls.
Check.	I can use division and subtraction to check my answer. $15 \div 3 = 5$ and $31 - 15 = 16$. Yes, I was correct!

Hints and tips

For some word problems you may also need to use the other operations – adding, subtracting or dividing – to find the answer.

Questions

1

a) A shop sells footballs for £4 each. How much does the shop get for selling 8 footballs?

b) The shop has four shelves each with 10 trainers on, and three shelves each with 8 trainers on. How many trainers are there altogether?

c) How much change would you get from £30 if you buy seven cricket balls at £3 each?

2

a) There are seven 5p coins and nine 10p coins in the till. How much money is this in total?

b) Some football players need new studs for their boots. Each player has a pair of boots and each boot needs 8 studs. How many studs are needed for 4 players' boots?

c) Sports bags come in three sizes. The large bag costs £8, the medium one costs £6 and the small one costs £5. What would be the total cost for five bags of each size?

CHALLENGE!

A dartboard costs £24, darts cost £2 each and a case that holds 3 darts costs £5.

Lee spends £57 on a board and some darts and cases.

What exactly did he buy?

Explore

Find out how much it costs to buy clothes and equipment for your favourite game or sport. Imagine you had £100 to spend. What would you buy?

Division and remainders

For some division problems, giving an answer with a remainder does not make sense. You may need to round up or down to the nearest whole number.

Chloe puts 29 holiday photos into a photo album. Each page holds 4 photos. What is the fewest number of pages that she could use?

Read the question, now read it again.

⬇

Decide your operations and units.

⬇

Approximate your answer.

⬇

Calculate.

⬇

Check.

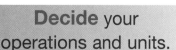

With division, I may have to either round up or down depending on the question.

How many 4s are in 29? That's dividing, but then I must round up to find the fewest number of pages needed.

I know that 28 divided by 4 is 7, so 29 divided by 4 will be 7r1.

$29 \div 4 = 7r1$; this means 7 full pages and 1 photo left over, so Chloe will need 8 pages for all the photos.

7 pages can hold 28 photos and 8 pages can hold 32 photos, so 29 photos will use 8 pages. I was correct!

Hints and tips

Sometimes you must round up, e.g. if asked questions such as *How many boxes (or coaches) would be needed?* Sometimes you must round down, e.g. if asked questions such as *How many are full?* or *How many could you buy?* Think carefully about which you need to do each time.

Questions

1

a) A minibus has room for 10 children. How many minibuses are needed to take 38 children?

b) Children get into groups of 5. How many groups of 5 can be made with 36 children?

c) Eggs come in boxes of six. How many full boxes can be made with 41 eggs?

2

a) A coach has room for 50 children. A total of 290 children are travelling by coach. All except one of the coaches are full. How many coaches are full?

b) Ryan puts 31 stickers into an empty album, filling each page as he goes. Each page holds 8 stickers. How many pages of the album are full?

c) Ellie has £50. How many £9 photo albums can she afford?

CHALLENGE!

Sam has 100 photos to put in albums. Which albums could she buy? How many would she need? How much would it cost?

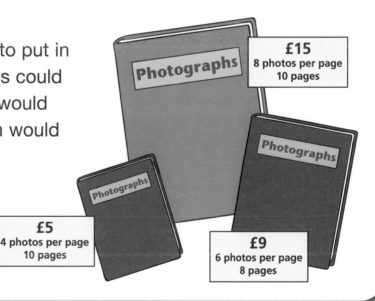

£15
8 photos per page
10 pages

£5
4 photos per page
10 pages

£9
6 photos per page
8 pages

Explore

Choose a foreign holiday destination and find out where the country is on the world map. Write five facts about the country, including its currency and whether it is in the northern or southern hemisphere.

Mixed calculations

It is important to be able to work out whether to add, subtract, multiply or divide to find the answer to a word problem.

In a field there are cows, sheep and horses. There are 10 more sheep than cows. There are half as many horses as cows. If there are 16 sheep, how many cows and how many horses are there?

Read the question, now read it again.

Decide your operations and units.

Approximate your answer.

Calculate.

Check.

Read slowly and carefully. What are you being asked to do?

I need to take 10 from 16 to find the number of cows and then halve the answer to find the number of horses.

16 – 10 is 6 and half of 6 is 3, so I think there are 6 cows and 3 horses.

16 – 10 = 6 so there are 6 cows. 6 ÷ 2 = 3 so there are 3 horses.

I'll re-read the question to make sure my answers fit. I'm right!

Hints and tips

Some questions will have just one step and others may have more. Think carefully about what to do and read the question carefully to the end.

Questions

1 a) A farmer has 8 chickens. If each lays 3 eggs, how many eggs is this altogether?

b) The farmer puts the eggs into boxes of 6. How many boxes this?

c) Jess the sheepdog rounds up 17 sheep and puts them in a field that already has 39 sheep in. How many sheep are in the field now?

2 a) There are twice as many goats as pigs and half as many pigs as geese. If there are 8 goats, how many geese are there?

b) In a field there are cows, sheep and horses. There are twice as many sheep as cows. There are half as many horses as cows. If there are 16 sheep, how many cows and how many horses are there?

c) A pond has a total of 52 ducks and ducklings. There are 10 more ducklings than ducks on the pond. How many ducklings are there?

CHALLENGE!

On Julian's farm there are 36 sheep, 40 cows, 6 pigs and 9 chickens. Write three questions of your own about Julian's farm for a partner to answer.

Explore

Find out how a sheep's fleece can be turned into wool. Can you find more information about carding and spinning? Draw and label some diagrams to show the process.

Fractions

In some word problems you may be asked to find fractions of numbers, such as one-quarter or two-fifths of a number.

Jo has a school photograph. In the photograph there are 32 children. One-quarter of the children are wearing skirts, the rest of the children are wearing trousers. How many are wearing trousers?

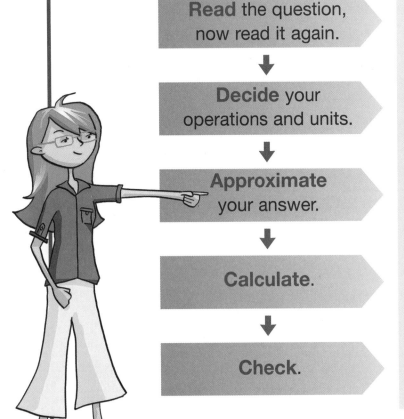

Read the question, now read it again.	Read slowly and carefully. What is the question asking?
Decide your operations and units.	I need to find one-quarter of 32 and take it away from 32 or I need to find three-quarters of 32.
Approximate your answer.	One-quarter of 32 is the same as $32 \div 4$, which is 8. $32 - 8$ is about 24, I think.
Calculate.	One-quarter of $32 = 8$ and $32 - 8 = 32 - 2 - 6 = 24$. So 24 children are wearing trousers.
Check.	I checked that three-quarters of 32 is 24. Yes, I was correct!

Hints and tips

When finding a fraction of a number, divide the number by the **denominator** (the bottom number) and multiply the answer by the **numerator** (the top number), for example, to find three-quarters of 32: $32 \div 4 \times 3 = 8 \times 3 = 24$.

Questions

1 a) In a school photo of 30 children, $\frac{1}{5}$ of them are wearing jumpers. How many are not wearing jumpers?

b) In a school photo of 27 children, $\frac{1}{3}$ of them are wearing ties. How many are not wearing ties?

c) In Sam's class of 30 children, $\frac{2}{5}$ of them are girls. How many are girls?

2 a) Only one-third of the children in Claire's class are boys. There are 10 boys. How many girls are there?

b) The 100 children in Tim's school are allowed to wear a skirt, trousers or shorts. If one-quarter of the children are wearing skirts and $\frac{7}{10}$ are wearing trousers, how many children are wearing shorts?

c) In a school photo of 28 children, $\frac{4}{7}$ of them are wearing short socks and $\frac{2}{7}$ are wearing long socks. The rest are wearing tights. How many are wearing tights?

CHALLENGE! Write some questions about these 24 children for a partner to answer.

Explore

Copy this Venn diagram onto a large piece of paper and draw some pictures of children that could be sorted into each section of the diagram.

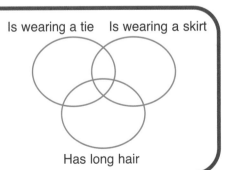

Is wearing a tie   Is wearing a skirt

Has long hair

Money

Questions about money can involve adding, subtracting, multiplying or dividing. You may be asked to work out how much change you should receive.

Cameron buys two packets of itching powder. Each packet costs 60p. He pays with a £2 coin. How much change does he get?

Read the question, now read it again.	Read slowly and carefully. What are you being asked to do?
Decide your operations and units.	I need to find two lots of 60p and take this from £2. That's subtracting.
Approximate your answer.	Two lots of 60p is 120p. Two pounds is two hundred pence. 200 – 120 = 80 perhaps?
Calculate.	2000p – 120p = 80p. Cameron would get 80p change.
Check.	I can check by counting on in tens from 120p to £2. It is 80p. Yes, I was correct!

Hints and tips

Remember to add the units on money questions: '£' for pounds or 'p' for pence.

Never use both at the same time! £5.30p

Questions

1 a) Cameron has saved some coins. He has one 10p, one 20p, one 50p and a £2 coin. How much does he have to spend at the novelty shop?

b) Cameron gives his sister Keeley the 50p coin and the 20p coin. How much does he have to spend now?

c) Keeley buys 2 pots of slime putty. They cost 28p each. How much does she spend on slime putty?

2 a) Cameron loves stink bombs! The stink bombs cost 35p for a box of 6. Cameron buys 18 stink bombs in total. How much does this cost him?

b) Keeley wants to buy an exploding golf ball to trick her dad! She has 14p left. The exploding golf ball costs 40p. How much more money does she need?

CHALLENGE!

The Sweet Shoppe sells a range of sweets for young wizards and witches.

Find at least three ways they could spend exactly £5.

Flavoured flies
25p per 100g

Crunchy cats
30p per 100g

Bogey biscuits
35p per 100g

Tasty toads
50p per 100g

Marshmallow mice
65p per 100g

Toffee toenails
75p per 100g

Explore

Find an image of a banknote and research the person depicted on it. Why are they important?

Place value

When solving place value problems it is important to know the value of each digit in a number. The number 264 has 2 hundreds, 6 tens and 4 ones.

Mrs Patel works in a bank. She is given some notes and coins to count. How much money does she have altogether if she has six £100 notes, four £10 notes and two pound coins?

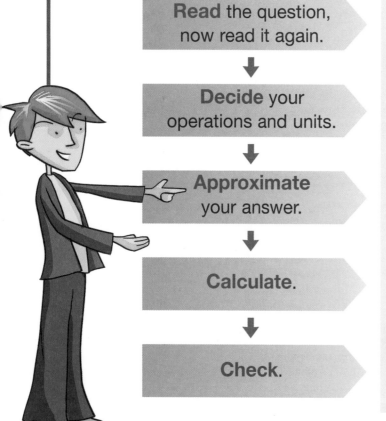

Read the question, now read it again.	I must find the sum of six £100 notes, four £10 notes and two £1 coins.
Decide your operations and units.	$(6 \times 100) + (4 \times 10) + (2 \times 1)$ The answer will be in pounds.
Approximate your answer.	$600 + 40 + 2$ I think the answer will be 642.
Calculate.	$600 + 40 + 2 = 642$, so the answer is £642.
Check.	I'll read the question again and make sure my answer makes sense. Yes, I was correct!

Hints and tips

H	T	U
5	5	5

Remember that the value of the hundreds digit (H) is ten times larger than the tens digit (T) and the tens digit is ten times larger than the units (ones) digit (U).

Questions

1
a) Mrs Patel is given some notes and coins to count. How much money does she have altogether if she has nine £100 notes and three pound coins?

b) How much money does she have in total if she has 17 pound coins?

c) How much money does she have in total if she has twenty £10 notes?

2
a) Mrs Patel puts £324 in a bag. She then puts in five more £10 notes. How much money is now in the bag?

b) A bag contains £748. Mrs Patel takes out four £100 notes and six pound coins. How much money is in the bag now?

c) A bag contains £904. Mrs Patel takes out two £10 notes. How much money is in the bag now?

CHALLENGE

A bag of money contains only £100 notes, £10 notes and £1 coins. The bag holds £206. What notes and coins could be in the bag? Write at least five different answers.

Remember that there might be more than six pound coins and perhaps less than two £100 notes.

Explore

In 1971, the notes and coins used in the United Kingdom changed to the coins used today. Previously, people used shillings, sixpences, half-crowns, old pennies and so on. Find out about the old coins and what they were worth. Write a short report about what you find.

Number lines and rounding

Numbers can be shown on number lines. This can help you to round them to the nearest 10 or 100. Be careful to check whether to round to the nearest 10 or to the nearest 100.

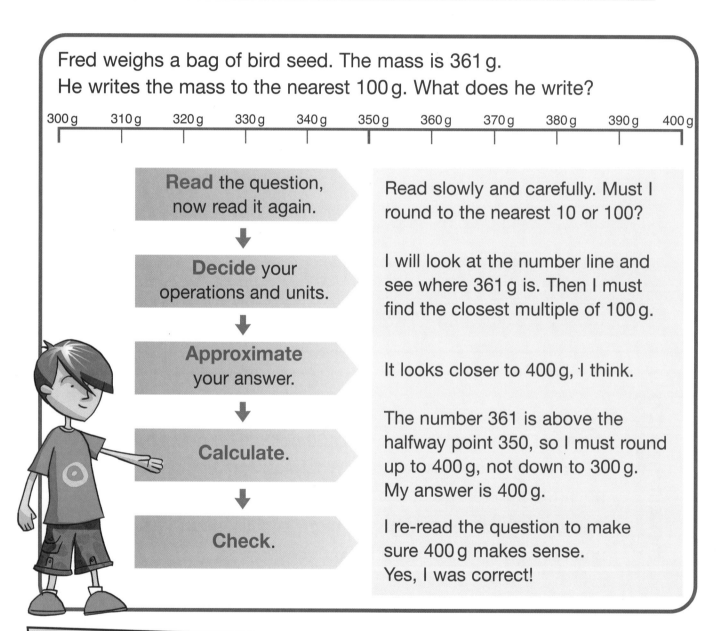

Fred weighs a bag of bird seed. The mass is 361 g.
He writes the mass to the nearest 100 g. What does he write?

300 g 310 g 320 g 330 g 340 g 350 g 360 g 370 g 380 g 390 g 400 g

Read the question, now read it again.

⬇

Decide your operations and units.

⬇

Approximate your answer.

⬇

Calculate.

⬇

Check.

Read slowly and carefully. Must I round to the nearest 10 or 100?

I will look at the number line and see where 361 g is. Then I must find the closest multiple of 100 g.

It looks closer to 400 g, I think.

The number 361 is above the halfway point 350, so I must round up to 400 g, not down to 300 g. My answer is 400 g.

I re-read the question to make sure 400 g makes sense.
Yes, I was correct!

Hints and tips

When rounding numbers to the nearest 10, the answer will be a multiple of 10, such as 60, 370, 450 etc. When rounding to the nearest 100, the answer will be a multiple of 100, such as 600, 3700, 4500 etc.

Questions

1 a) Fred weighs a bag of peanuts. The mass is 584 g. He writes the mass to the nearest 10 g. What does he write?

| 500 g | 510 g | 520 g | 530 g | 540 g | 550 g | 560 g | 570 g | 580 g | 590 g | 600 g |

b) A bag weighs 300 g when rounded to the nearest 10 g. Which of the arrows shows the bag's mass?

| 250 g | 260 g | 270 g | 280 g | 290 g | 300 g | 310 g | 320 g | 330 g | 340 g | 350 g |

252 g   280 g   296 g   310 g

2 a) A number when rounded to the nearest 10 is 850 and when rounded to the nearest 100 is 800. What is the smallest whole number it could be?

| 800 | 810 | 820 | 830 | 840 | 850 | 860 | 870 | 880 | 890 | 900 |

b) Fred rounds the mass of a bag to the nearest 100 g and gets the answer 600 g. He then rounds the mass to the nearest 10 g and gets the answer 650 g. Which of these is his bag?

655 g   660 g   646 g   651 g

| 600 g | 610 g | 620 g | 630 g | 640 g | 650 g | 660 g | 670 g | 680 g | 690 g | 700 g |

CHALLENGE!

A whole number when rounded to the nearest 10 is 600 and when rounded to the nearest 100 is also 600. What is the largest and smallest number that it could be?

Explore

Time lines are sometimes used to show when events happened long ago. Draw a time line of events in your own life to show when special things happened.

Measures – length

For questions about length you may need to add, subtract, multiply or divide. Remember to give the correct unit in your answer, such as mm, cm, m or km.

Simon cycles 2000 m every day for six days and then 3 km on Sunday. How many kilometres does he cycle in total that week?

Read the question, now read it again.	Read slowly and carefully. What are you being asked to do?
Decide your operations and units.	I'll find six lots of 2000 m and then add on 3 km, but I must be careful with the units. I'll change the 2000 m to 2 km and work in kilometres.
Approximate your answer.	If Simon cycled 2 km for seven days it would be 14 km, but he cycles an extra kilometre on Sunday, so I think the answer is 15 km.
Calculate.	6 × 2 km = 12 km 12 km + 3 km = 15 km
Check.	I'll check in metres … 6 × 2000 m + 3000 m = 15 000 m = 15 km. Yes, I was correct!

Hints and tips

Remember that 10 mm = 1 cm, 100 cm = 1 m and 1000 m = 1 km. Always change the measurements so that they are in the same unit.

Questions

1 a) Simon is 125 cm tall. His mum is 1.5 m tall.
What is the difference between their heights?

b) A 2p coin is about 2.5 cm wide. If two 2p coins are touching
side-by-side, what is the width across in millimetres?

c) Simon's house is 1500 m from his school. Simon cycled to
school and home again. How many kilometres did he cycle?

2 a) Kylie has five new pencils. Each pencil is 18 cm long.
Kylie puts them touching end-to-end in a line.
What is the length of the line in centimetres?

b) A piece of ribbon is two metres long. I cut some off.
It is now 122 cm long. How much did I cut off?

c) From the floor, a spider climbs 30 mm up a wall.
It then climbs 9 cm higher before dropping 20 mm.
How far from the floor is the spider now?

CHALLENGE! If I have several sticks that are 4 cm or 7 cm long, what
different lengths can I measure with the sticks?

Explore

Use a tape measure,
or some string and a ruler, to find your
own body measurements. Draw and
label a diagram like the one shown with
your measurements.

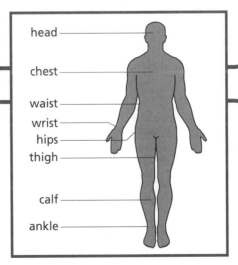

head
chest
waist
wrist
hips
thigh
calf
ankle

Measures – capacity

When solving capacity problems you may need to read a scale and then add, subtract, multiply or divide.

A scientist pours some liquid into this jug. For his experiment he needs three-quarters of a litre. How much more liquid does he need?

Read the question, now read it again.

How much is three-quarters of a litre? It is the same as 750 ml.

Decide your operations and units.

I need to read the scale and subtract the reading from 750.

Approximate your answer.

The scale shows halfway between 200 ml and 300 ml, that is 250 ml.
750 – 250 = 500

Calculate.

The scale shows 250 ml.
750 ml – 250 ml = 500 ml

Check.

I can add 500 ml and 250 ml to see if it is three-quarters of a litre. It is!

Hints and tips

Remember that 1000 millilitres (1000 ml) is the same as one litre (1 l), 500 ml is half a litre and 250 ml is one-quarter of a litre.

Questions

1
a) How much liquid is in this tube?

b) The scientist pours an extra 19 ml into this tube. How much much more does he need to make 50 ml?

c) A small spoon can hold 5 ml of liquid when full. How many full spoonfuls of acid can the scientist take from a bowl containing 48 ml of acid?

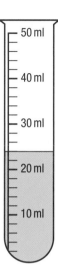

2
a) A jug holds 650 ml of liquid and a cup holds 225 ml. The liquid from the jug and cup is poured into a litre bowl. How much more liquid is needed to fill the litre bowl?

b) For an experiment a scientist needs one-fifth of the liquid in this container. How many millilitres does he need?

CHALLENGE
A small spoon can hold 5 ml and a large spoon can hold 12 ml. The scientist has a large bowl of water and an empty bowl. Which amounts between 20 ml and 30 ml can the scientist measure using the two spoons and how would he do it?

Explore

Get a large bowl of water. Carefully balance a matchstick on the water's surface. Now add a small amount of soap and watch the matchstick shoot across the water! Find out why this happens and make an information sheet about what you found out!

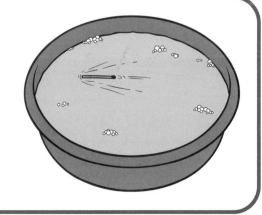

Measures – mass

Questions about mass are about how heavy something is, such as 100 g or 24 kg. We use different types of scales to weigh things, such as bathroom or kitchen scales.

The total mass of these three parcels is 2 kg. Two have the same mass and the smaller one weighs 200 g. What is the mass of one of the larger ones?

200 g

Read the question, now read it again.

Read slowly and carefully. What are you being asked to do?

Decide your operations and units.

I must subtract 200 g from 2 kg (which is 2000 g) and then halve that answer.

Approximate your answer.

Half of 2 kg is 1 kg, so each large parcel will be less than 1 kg.

Calculate.

2000 g – 200 g = 1800 g
1800 g ÷ 2 = 900 g

Check.

I can add 900 g, 900 g and 200 g to check it is 2000 g. I was correct!

Hints and tips

Remember that 1000 grams (1000 g) is the same as one kilogram (1 kg).

Questions

1 a) Three identical parcels each weigh 125 g. What is the total mass of the three parcels?

b) One parcel weighs 375 g. A second parcel weighs 225 g heavier. What is the total mass of the two parcels?

c) A parcel weighs 750 g. A larger parcel is three times heavier than this one. What is the mass of the larger parcel?

2 a) A larger parcel is four times heavier than a smaller one. The smaller one weighs 150 g. What is the mass of the larger parcel?

b) Jo has three parcels that have a total mass of 1 kilogram. One parcel weighs 0.5 kg and another weighs 150 g. How heavy is the third parcel?

c) Two identical parcels each weigh $\frac{1}{2}$ kg. A larger parcel weighs 250 g more than one of them. What is the total mass of the parcels?

CHALLENGE. Make up three parcel questions of your own for a partner to answer.

Explore

Imagine you have a special parcel to send to the other side of the world. What is in the parcel? What size and shape is it? Who are you sending it to and why? Write a story about your parcel and its journey.

Time

To solve time problems you need to be able to read the time on a clock-face (analogue clock) and on a digital clock.

At a cinema, a film starts at the time shown on this clock.

The film is two and a half hours long. What time does the film finish?

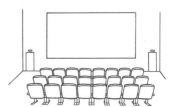

Read the question, now read it again.

⬇

Decide your operations and units.

⬇

Approximate your answer.

⬇

Calculate.

⬇

Check.

Read carefully and look at the clock. What do you need to do?

The clock shows 'twenty to four'. I must count forwards 2 hours and 30 minutes.

'Twenty to four' is 3:40. Two hours later is 5:40, so the film will finish just after 6 o'clock.

Using a number line, 30 minutes after 5:40 is 6:10.

```
          20        10      = 30 minutes
5:40            6:00  6:10
```
The film finishes at 6:10.

I can count back from my answer to make sure.

Hints and tips

There are 60 minutes in a whole hour, 30 minutes in half an hour and 15 minutes in a quarter of an hour. Remember that for digital times the hour is written first, so 4:15 is 'quarter past four'.

Questions

1 a) A film called *Creepers* starts at six thirty.
It finishes at the time shown on this clock.
How long is the film in hours and minutes?

b) The adverts before a film last for twenty minutes. They start
showing at 3:45. What time do they end? Write your answer
in digital time.

c) The film *Star Battle* starts at twenty-five to seven
and finishes at 8:45. How long is the film?

2 a) The digital clocks show the start and end
times of a film. How many hours and minutes
is the film?

b) What is the length of the film in minutes?

c) A film lasts for 70 minutes. It finishes at 7:30.
What time did it start?

CHALLENGE!

This chart shows the times and lengths of
some films at a cinema. Make up three
questions of your own about the information.

Film	Length	Start time
Gone with the Breeze	2 hrs 15 minutes	6:20
Shreeek	1 hr 50 minutes	4:30
Robin Wood	150 minutes	5:00

Explore

Think of your favourite film.
Imagine you were writing about the film for a
local newspaper. Write a summary of the
storyline and include information about the film's
length, its price at the local cinema and so on.

2-D shapes

2-D shapes are two-dimensional flat shapes. You need to remember the names of common shapes and their properties, for example, how many sides, vertices (corners), right angles or lines of symmetry they have.

Deepa takes the red triangle and folds it in half. Which shapes show the triangle after it has been folded? There may be more than one answer.

A B C D E

Read the question, now read it again.

↓

Decide your operations and units.

↓

Approximate your answer.

↓

Calculate.

↓

Check.

Read slowly and carefully. What are you being asked to do?

I need to work out which of the shapes can be made by folding the red triangle in half.

I'm sure that A is possible, but what about the other shapes?

I think that E can also be made. So my answers are A and E.

I'll check each of the other shapes again.

Hints and tips

Quadrilaterals are shapes with four straight sides. When a symmetrical shape is folded along its line of symmetry it is folded exactly in half.

Questions

1 a) Deepa takes the red hexagon and folds it in half. Which of the shapes shown can be made by folding it in half? There may be more than one answer.

 A B C D E

b) Leroy draws a quadrilateral onto dotty paper. The shape has one right angle and no lines of symmetry. His shape is one of the shapes below. Which is his shape?

A   B   C   D   E   F

2 a) Elisha draws a quadrilateral with two lines of symmetry. It has four right angles. What is the name of this shape?

b) What two shapes can be made by folding a square in half?

c) Joe counts the number of lines of symmetry in a square and in a rectangle. He adds the two numbers together. What is his answer?

CHALLENGE.

A pentomino is a shape made from touching five squares. Use squared paper to draw as many pentominoes as you can. Two are shown here. How many symmetrical pentominoes can you find?

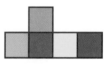

Explore

Many of the names of our 2-D shapes come from Greek numbers. 'Pende' means five in Greek and this is where the word 'pentagon' comes from. Find out how to count from one to ten in Greek.

3-D shapes

3-D shapes are three-dimensional shapes that you can hold. When solving 3-D shape problems you need to remember the names of common shapes and their properties, such as how many faces, edges and vertices (corners) they have.

Lia sorts some 3-D shapes. She puts the shapes with at least one triangular face into one group. She has made one mistake. Which shape is in the wrong group? Give its correct name.

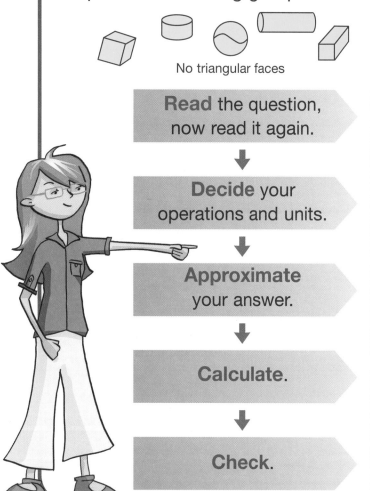

No triangular faces

At least one triangular face

Read the question, now read it again.

⬇

Decide your operations and units.

⬇

Approximate your answer.

⬇

Calculate.

⬇

Check.

Read slowly and carefully. What are you being asked to do?

I need to look for a shape in the first group that has one or more triangular faces or one in the second group with no triangular faces.

I have to imagine holding each shape.

I think it is the cone as the cone only has a circular face and a curved face.

I can check all the other shapes to make sure. Yes, I'm correct!

Hints and tips

A prism has the same cross-section along its whole length. Prisms include cubes, cuboids and cylinders, and triangular, pentagonal and hexagonal prisms. A vertex is a corner.

Questions

1 a) In Lia's diagram into which group would you put a hexagonal prism?

b) In Lia's diagram into which group would you put this cuboid?

2 a) Lia sorts some 3-D shapes into a Venn diagram. She has made one mistake. Which shape is in the wrong group? Give its correct name.

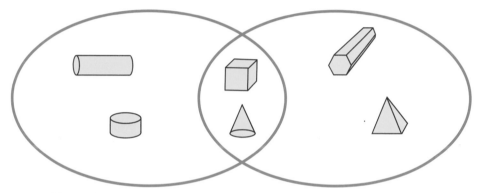

Has at least one circular face   Has at least one vertex

b) In which part of the diagram would a cuboid be placed?

CHALLENGE! Draw your own Venn diagram with different headings, such as *Is a prism* or *Has at least one rectangular face* and sort some shapes of your own.

Explore

Maurits Escher was a famous Dutch artist who drew many optical illusions. Find some of his pictures and write some notes about them. You could find more about him at http://www.worldofescher.com/gallery/.

Position and direction

To solve problems about position and direction you will need to know the compass points: north, south, east and west.

A counter is put on D3. It is then moved 2 squares east and 3 squares north. Where does the counter end up?

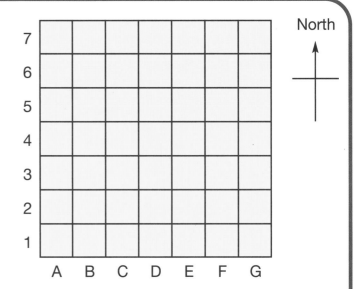

Read the question, now read it again.	Read slowly and carefully. In which direction will the counter be moved?
Decide your operations and units.	I need to follow the instructions carefully.
Approximate your answer.	East is to the right and north is up.
Calculate.	I follow the instructions on the grid and reach F6.
Check.	I can work backwards, doing the opposite each time, to see if I reach the start. Yes, I was correct!

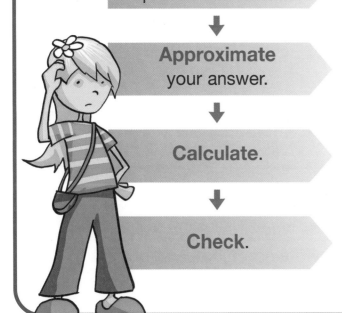

Hints and tips

Make sure you remember that west is left.

Questions

1

a) A counter is put on square G5. It is then moved 6 squares west and 1 square south. Where does the counter end up?

b) A counter is put on square A4. It is then moved 3 squares north and 5 squares east. Where does the counter end up?

c) A counter is put on square E1. It is then moved 4 squares north and 3 squares west. Where does the counter end up?

2

a) Write a set of instructions for a route going from square G1 to square B4.

b) Write a set of instructions for a route going from square A6 to square F2.

CHALLENGE.

Write a set of your own instructions to help someone move through this maze or draw one of your own on squared paper and write instructions for a partner to follow.

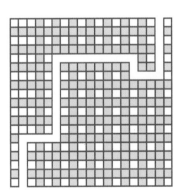

Explore

Go online and see if you can find how to make a compass using a bowl of water, a magnet and a needle. See if you can make your own.

Tables

Make sure that you understand what information is shown in a table or tally chart. For this type of problem you need to work out which numbers are important and sometimes find totals or differences.

This table shows the number of arrows that landed in each part of a target board.

How many arrows landed on the board in total?

Colour	Tally	Frequency
Red	IIII	4
Yellow	ЖЖ	
Blue	ЖЖ II	
Green	ЖЖ I	
Orange	III	

Read the question, now read it again.

Look at the tally marks in the table. What do they show?

Decide your operations and units.

I must work out the frequencies and add them together.

Approximate your answer.

There look to be over 20 marks.

Calculate.

4 + 5 + 7 + 6 + 3 = 25, so the answer is 25 arrows.

Check.

I can add the numbers in a different order to make sure.

Hints and tips

The headings of the table tell you what information it is trying to show. Tally marks are grouped in fives. Complete the frequency column of the table before answering the questions.

Questions

1 a) Look at the table opposite. How many more arrows landed in the blue section than the yellow section?

b) How many fewer landed in the yellow, orange and red sections than in the green and blue sections?

2 This table shows another game of arrows. Compare the two tables.

Colour	Tally	Frequency
Red	JHT III	
Yellow	JHT	
Blue	JHT JHT IIII	
Green	JHT JHT JHT IIII	
Orange	JHT	

a) How many more arrows landed in the red section in this game than in the game opposite?

b) What was the total number of arrows that landed on the board?

c) How many more arrows landed on the board in this game than in the game opposite?

CHALLENGE■

In another game, 50 arrows landed on the target board. Draw your own table to show how many arrows could have landed in each section. Then write some questions of your own about the information.

Explore

Find out about and write your own story about Robin Hood, his friends and some of his adventures.

Graphs, charts and diagrams

Data handling questions will ask you to look at a graph, chart or diagram and use the data to answer the questions. A pictogram shows information using pictures.

A class drew a pictogram to show how often their teacher got cross in school each day in a week.

How many times did the teacher get cross on Thursday?

How often Mrs X gets cross

Monday	
Tuesday	
Wednesday	
Thursday	
Friday	
Saturday	
Sunday	

Key: = Teacher getting cross twice

Read the question, now read it again.

→

Decide your operations and units.

→

Approximate your answer.

→

Calculate.

→

Check.

Look at the key carefully. What does each picture represent?

The pictogram is telling me how many times the teacher got cross in school each day in a week.

I have to look at all the information that is given to me.

There are $2\frac{1}{2}$ pictures for Thursday. Each picture stands for the teacher getting cross twice, so that is five times altogether.

I can count up in twos to check. Yes, I was correct!

Hints and tips

Look at the key of the pictogram very carefully.
The key here shows that each picture represents
two units or the teacher getting cross twice.

Questions

1 a) How many times did the teacher get cross on Tuesday?

   b) How many times did the teacher get cross on Friday?

   c) On which day did the teacher get cross only once?

2 a) On how many more occasions did the teacher get cross on Friday than on Monday?

   b) How many times did the teacher get cross during the whole week?

   c) Why do you think the pictogram shows that the teacher didn't get cross on Saturday or Sunday?

CHALLENGE!

Think about what it would mean if the key on this pictogram was changed so that it said:

 = Teacher getting cross ten times

How many times would it mean that the teacher had got cross each day? How many times would it mean the teacher got cross during the whole week?

Explore

Look online and in magazines or newspapers for examples of pictograms. Can you work out what they are trying to show?

Answers

Patterns and sequences
(Pages 10–11)
Questions:
1 a) 21 cm
b) 1000 g
c) 27
2 a) 26   17   11
b) 1996 and 2008

Addition and subtraction
(Pages 12–13)
Questions:
1 a) 63
b) 36
c) 18
2 a) 42
b) £9
c) 11p
Challenge:
All even numbers.

Multiplication
(Pages 14–15)
Questions:
1 a) £32
b) 64 trainers
c) £9
2 a) £1.25
b) 64 studs
c) £95
Challenge:
1 board, 9 darts and
3 cases.

Division and remainders
(Pages 16–17)
Questions:
1 a) 4 minibuses
b) 7 groups
c) 6 boxes
2 a) 5 coaches
b) 3 pages
c) 5 albums

Mixed calculations
(Pages 18–19)
Questions:
1 a) 24 eggs
b) 4 boxes
c) 56 sheep
2 a) 8 geese
b) 8 cows, 4 horses
c) 31 ducklings

Fractions
(Pages 20–21)
Questions:
1 a) 24 children
b) 18 children
c) 12 are girls
2 a) 20 girls
b) 5 children
c) 4 children

Money
(Pages 22–23)
Questions:
1 a) £2.80
b) £2.10
c) 56p
2 a) £1.05
b) 26p

Place value
(Pages 24–25)
Questions:
1 a) £903
b) £17
c) £200
2 a) £374
b) £342
c) £884

Number lines and rounding
(Pages 26–27)
Questions:
1 a) 580 g
b) 296 g
2 a) 845
b) 646 g
Challenge:
Largest 604; smallest 595.

Measures – length
(Pages 28–29)
Questions:
1 a) 25 cm
b) 50 mm
c) 3 km
2 a) 90 cm
b) 78 cm
c) 10 cm
Challenge:
Example answers:
$1 = 4 + 4 - 7$
$2 = 7 + 7 - 4 - 4 - 4$
$3 = 7 - 4$ etc.

Measures – capacity
(Pages 30–31)
Questions:
1 a) 24 ml
b) 7 ml
c) 9 spoonfuls
2 a) 125 ml
b) 16 ml
Challenge:
Example answers:
20 = 5 + 5 + 5 + 5
i.e. 4 × 5 ml spoonfuls
21 = 12 + 12 + 12 – 5 – 5 – 5 i.e. 3 × 12 ml
spoonfuls subtract 3 × 5 ml spoonfuls
22 = 12 + 5 + 5
23 = 4 lots of 12 – 5 lots of 5 etc.

Measures – mass
(Pages 32–33)
Questions:
1 a) 375 g
b) 600 g
c) 2250 g
2 a) 600 g
b) 350 g
c) 1.75 kg = 1750 g

Time
(Pages 34–35)
Questions:
1 a) 2 hours and 30 minutes
b) 4:05
c) 2 hours and 10 minutes
2 a) 1 hour 5 minutes
b) 65 minutes
c) 6:20

2-D shapes
(Pages 36–37)
Questions:
1 a) A
b) E
2 a) Rectangle
b) Rectangle, triangle.
c) 6
Challenge:

3-D shapes
(Pages 38–39)
Questions:
1 a) No triangular faces
b) No triangular faces
2 a) Cube
b) Has at least one vertex

Position and direction
(Pages 40–41)
Questions:
1 a) A4
b) F7
c) B5
2 a) Any suitable directions
b) Any suitable directions

Tables
(Pages 42–43)
Questions:
1 a) 2
b) 4
2 a) 4
b) 51
c) 26

Graphs, charts and diagrams
(Pages 44–45)
Questions:
1 a) 3
b) 8
c) Wednesday
2 a) 6
b) 19
c) It was the weekend.

Notes